HEAD GAMES
LOCKE & KEY
VOLUME 2

WRITTEN BY
JOE HILL

ART BY
GABRIEL RODRIGUEZ

Written by: Joe Hill

Art by: Gabriel Rodriguez

Colors by: Jay Fotos

Letters by: Robbie Robbins

Series Edited by: Chris Ryall

Collection Edited by: Justin Eisinger

Collection Designed by: Robbie Robbins

Locke & Key created by Joe Hill and Gabriel Rodriguez

For international rights, contact licensing@idwpublishing.com

ISBN: 978-1-60010-761-0

23 22 21 20   14 15 16 17

IDW

www.IDWPUBLISHING.com

Chris Ryall, President & Publisher/CCO • Cara Morrison, Chief Financial Officer • Matthew Ruzicka, Chief Accounting Officer • David Hedgecock, Associate Publisher • John Barber, Editor-in-Chief • Justin Eisinger, Editorial Director, Graphic Novels and Collections • Scott Dunbier, Director, Special Projects • Jerry Bennington, VP of New Product Development • Lorelei Bunjes, VP of Technology & Information Services • Jud Meyers, Sales Director • Anna Morrow, Marketing Director • Tara McCrillis, Director of Design & Production • Mike Ford, Director of Operations • Rebekah Cahalin, General Manager
Ted Adams and Robbie Robbins, IDW Founders

Facebook: facebook.com/idwpublishing • Twitter: @idwpublishing • YouTube: youtube.com/idwpublishing
Tumblr: tumblr.idwpublishing.com • Instagram: instagram.com/idwpublishing

introduction
by Warren Ellis

The thing I hate most about Joe Hill is that he's cleverer than I am, and therefore has things in his head that are better than the things in my head, so what I need to do is fashion a key of some kind, very sharp, and jam it into his neck, just below the base of his skull, and twist it hard until the top of his head opens, and then rummage around in there for the clever bits, pick them out, and stuff them into a bottle, which I will fill with wine, allowing his clever bits to suffuse into the liquid, and so I will drink the then-fortified wine filled with nutritious Joe Hill headbits, and therefore will be clever enough to one day come up with the wonderful metaphorical conceit of keys to open our heads and reveal all we hide away in that dark little space, except that that's an idea Joe Hill's already had and I crudely ripped it off when I tooled my own key that I shoved into the back of Joe Hill's head, and it's not a special metaphorical magic key, it's just an old doorkey, so now there's Joe Hill's head with this manky old key that I filed a point on sticking out of the back of his neck, and he's actually made kind of a mess, and the worst thing I suppose is that he fairly obviously won't be writing any more *LOCKE & KEY* comics, which is a bloody (hah) shame because these comics are really remarkably good, among the best-written comics I've seen in the last two years, which I guess is because Joe Hill's cleverer than I am and that's why he had to die.

Sorry.

Warren Ellis
Not Telling You My Location Oh No
July 2009

WHEN YOU SAID "LET'S GO STUDY DOWN BY THE CREEK," I DIDN'T THINK YOU REALLY MEANT "LET'S GO STUDY."

UH-HUH. HANG ON. I'VE GOT THE PERFECT OPENING HERE.

I'D LIKE TO SEE MR. FARMER TRY AND DISMISS *THIS* AS INADEQUATE FOR MY DISSERTATION. HE'S THE MOST RACIST SHITBIRD IN THIS WHOLE UNIVERSITY.

PROFESSOR FARMER IS BLACK.

SO?

WHAT DO YOU THINK OF THIS? "FROM MACBETH TO HAMLET TO CAESAR, SHAKESPEARE'S GHOSTS ARRIVE TO STAIN HIS PROTAGONISTS WITH UNBEARABLE KNOWLEDGE, TO DRIVE THEM TO *ACT*, AND TO—"

I'M GOING IN THE WATER.

I'M GOING TO SWIM TO THE BOTTOM OF THE RIVER AND STAY DOWN UNTIL YOU RESCUE ME OR I DROWN, WHICHEVER COMES FIRST.

WHERE DID YOU GO?

LOVECRAFT, MASSACHUSETTS. NOW.

I WOULD'VE RETIRED BY NOW IF YOU DIDN'T DIE ON ME. THE PLAN WAS TO BOTH GET OUT AT THE SAME TIME.

GO TO AMALFI, WHERE WE WENT FOR OUR HONEYMOON.

THE GHOST CODE
Joseph Elmore Ridgeway III

I ALWAYS THOUGHT WE'D HAVE TIME FOR ITALY.

MEMORY-
GHOSTS: *Inaction is a*
CHOICE

STAY, ILLUSION! IF THOU HAST ANY SOUND OR USE OF VOICE, SPEAK TO ME!

BUT I LIKE HAVING YOU NEAR. I CAN CLOSE MY EYES AND IMAGINE YOU'RE WAITING FOR ME IN THE FACULTY LOUNGE AND IN A MOMENT WE'LL HAVE OUR MORNING COFFEE TOGETHER.

I SHOULD'VE GOT OUT A WHILE AGO BUT I CAN'T LEAVE. YOU WORKED HERE, TOO. THIS WAS OUR PLACE.

SOME PEOPLE WOULD'VE WANTED TO GET AWAY. TOO MANY GHOSTS.

BESIDES, HOW OFTEN DID I SAY I WOULD LOVE, JUST ONCE IN MY LIFE, TO SEE A REAL, HONEST-TO-GOD...

...GHOST.

THE MOMENT I SEE HIM I'M TELLING MYSELF "IT ISN'T HIM, YOU OLD FOOL." I'M TELLING MYSELF "DON'T BE SENILE."

I'VE TAUGHT MAYBE 8,000 STUDENTS OVER THE LAST FORTY YEARS. SOME OF THEM ARE BOUND TO LOOK LIKE OTHERS, AND IT ISN'T, IT JUST CAN'T BE—

LUKE?

AND AT THE SOUND OF HIS NAME HE LOOKS BACK. HE CAN'T HELP HIMSELF. CAN ANYONE?

LUCAS DON CARAVAGGIO. ONLY THERE WAS SOME OTHER NAME FOR YOU, WASN'T THERE? WHAT DID THE KIDS CALL YOU?

DOGG? NO. DIGGER? DIZZY?

DOESN'T MATTER. NOT IMPORTANT.

BERNADETTE TELLS ME HE TRANSFERRED IN TWO WEEKS AGO FROM A SCHOOL IN TEXAS. SHE SAYS HIS NAME IS ZACK WELLS.

YOU OKAY, JOE?

UNH.

A MOMENT LATER HE WALKS ON, AS IF SOMETHING DIDN'T JUST HAPPEN.

HE'D HAVE TO BE, WHAT—35? 40 NOW?

BUT THERE HE IS. LIKE IT HASN'T BEEN ONE DAY SINCE HE DISAPPEARED.

HIM AND THE OTHERS.

I DON'T KNOW WHAT TO MAKE OF HIM WALKING AROUND WITH TYLER LOCKE, NOT AFTER WHAT THE LOCKE BOY HAS BEEN THROUGH IN THE LAST YEAR. THE GHOST OF HIS FATHER'S BEST FRIEND. IT CAN'T BE A COINCIDENCE, BUT I CAN'T IMAGINE WHAT IT MEANS.

THAT'S ALMOST THE MOST DISTURBING PART. *ALMOST.*

THE MOST DISTURBING PART IS THAT BERNIE SAYS HE'S STAYING WITH ELLIE WHEDON. WHEN I HEAR THAT I FEEL SICK INTO MY NERVE ENDINGS.

OF COURSE HE'D BE STAYING WITH HER.

WHAT ARE THEY TALKING ABOUT, I WONDER?

WE GOT PROBLEMS.

LUKE? I'M HOME.

DON'T CALL ME THAT. YOU HAVE TO PRACTICE CALLING ME ZACK OR YOU'RE GOING TO GET US INTO TROUBLE.

SORRY. IT'S JUST... YOU DON'T LOOK ANY DIFFERENT THAN—AH!

THIS ISN'T EASY, YOU KNOW. IT WAS EASY IN THE WELLHOUSE. BUT IT'S GETTING HARDER. IT HURTS A LITTLE NOW.

PLEASE. STOP.

I DON'T LIKE IT, LUKE.

I SAID YOU NEED TO STOP CALLING ME LUKE. WHAT DID I USED TO TELL YOU? UGLY GIRLS CAN'T AFFORD TO BE STUPID, TOO.

GOOD OL' MR. RIDGEWAY RECOGNIZED ME TODAY. THAT OLD FUCK. SHOULDN'T HE BE DEAD OR SENILE BY NOW?

WILL. YOU. LOWER. YOUR. VOICE?

MY SON IS IN THE NEXT ROOM.

RATIONS ARE BEING BEAMED IN. HOPE YOU LIKE STRAWBERRY SMOOTHIES.

YES SIR, THAT IS AFFIRMATIVE!

HE DOESN'T UNDERSTAND—

YOU HAVE NO IDEA WHAT HE UNDERSTANDS. CLOSE THE DOOR.

NO TRANSMISSIONS, SIR! WE HAVE REASON TO BELIEVE THE SIGNAL FROM HQ HAS BEEN CUT OFF.

NEXT ON B*A*D*G*E... WE GO INSIDE THE MAJOR CRIMES DIVISION OF BOSTON P.D.!

COPY THAT. I DON'T TRUST. THE NEW HUMAN. HE MAY BE A... REPLICANT.

WHAT'S ON, DUDE? GOT YOUR POWER DRINK.

... AFTER THEY'VE SERVED AS EVIDENCE, AND WE KNOW WE WON'T NEED TO PRODUCE THEM FOR AN APPEAL, WE SEND THEM TO THE FOUNDRY TO BE MELTED DOWN. AT THIS TIME WE HAVE OVER A THOUSAND ILLEGAL GUNS RANGING FROM AUTOMATIC WEAPONS TO...

14

I ALWAYS THOUGHT I'D DIE FIRST.

THREE PIPES A NIGHT. I ALWAYS THOUGHT IF ONE OF US WOULD GET CANCER—

YEARBOOK 1968 LOVECRAFT ACADEMY BE TRUE TO T

I'M STILL MAD AT YOU. YOU HAD NO RIGHT TO GO AWAY AND LEAVE ME. I HOPE YOU KNOW THAT, WHEREVER YOU ARE.

BUT I DIDN'T GET THIS BOOK DOWN TO LOOK AT YOU.

CALLIOPE RIDGEWAY
Head of Admissions

THERE HE IS. NO DOUBT ABOUT IT.

LUCAS CARAVAGGIO AND RENDELL LOCKE. BUTCH AND SUNDANCE. WHAT A PAIR THOSE TWO WERE.

I STILL REMEMBER THE DAY CARAVAGGIO DISAPPEARED, ALONG WITH THE TOPHER GIRL AND CHO. AND OF COURSE WHAT HAPPENED TO ERIN VOSS. AWFUL. JUST AWFUL. WORST DAY IN THE HISTORY OF THIS SCHOOL. RENDELL WAS DEVASTATED. NEVER THE SAME.

IT OCCURS TO ME IF CARAVAGGIO HAS COME BACK, IT MUST BE TO WATCH OVER RENDELL LOCKE'S CHILDREN, WHO HAVE ALREADY BEEN THROUGH SO MUCH. I GRASP AT THE THOUGHT, DESPERATELY WANTING IT TO BE TRUE.

LOVECRAFT SENIOR DRAMA - *THE TEMPEST*
From Left: MARK CHO, LUCAS CARAVAGGIO, ELLIE WHEDON, RENDELL LOCKE, KIM TOPHER, ERIN VOSS.
Far Right: Professor JOE RIDGEWAY - Director.

THE TEMPEST. WHAT A PLAY THAT WAS. NEVER SEEN ANYTHING LIKE IT. IT WAS...

MR. RIDGEWAY.

IT'S NEARLY FIRST PERIOD. YOU HAVE A LESSON TO TEACH

I BELIEVE I HAVE ONE TO TEACH RIGHT NOW.

OH, HA-HA.

WE TALKED ABOUT WHAT IT WOULD BE LIKE, FOR ONE OF US TO LOSE THE OTHER.

BUT THAT'S NOT HOW IT WORKS. YOU DON'T LOSE ANYONE. YOU AREN'T LOST. I CLOSE MY EYES AND THERE YOU ARE.

I SHOULDN'T BE DOING THIS.

THERE ARE RULES TO PROTECT STUDENT PRIVACY.

BUT CALLIE... YOU TAUGHT ME A HEALTHY DISRESPECT FOR RULES.

BESIDES. AT MY AGE YOU CAN PRETEND TO BE A LITTLE DOTTY AND GET AWAY WITH MOST ANYTHING.

A WHITE GIRL FROM THE SOUTH LOVING A BLACK MAN IN 1967. MY GOD, YOU'RE LUCKY YOU DIDN'T GET US BOTH KILLED.

SAYS HERE HE WAS ON THE DEAN'S LIST FOR ACADEMIC ACHIEVEMENT AND CAPTAIN OF THEIR FENCING TEAM. WASN'T LUCAS CARAVAGGIO ALSO... BUT THAT DOESN'T PROVE ANYTHING.

THEN THERE'S A PERSONAL NOTE FROM ELLIE, IDENTIFYING HIM AS A COUSIN AND EXPLAINING HE'LL BE STAYING WITH HER. I DIDN'T KNOW YOU HAD KIN OUT WEST, ELLIE.

THERE'S A NUMBER FOR THE SCHOOL HE TRANSFERRED OUT OF IN TEXAS. A PART OF ME DOESN'T WANT TO CALL. A PART OF ME IS AFRAID TO... AFRAID OF WHAT I MIGHT FIND OUT.

HELLO, I'M WITH THE ADMISSIONS DEPARTMENT AT LOVECRAFT ACADEMY. I HAD A QUESTION—

—SURE, I CAN HOLD.

HI. THIS IS MISTER, ER, MR. WILLIAMS, WITH ADMISSIONS. HERE AT LOVECRAFT ACADEMY.

I'M JUST MISSING SOME PAPER ON THIS TRANSFER STUDENT OF YOURS.

I DON'T HAVE ANY RECORDS FOR... COULD YOU HANG ON?

HUNH.

I'M BACK. I JUST HAD A QUESTION ABOUT YOUR TRANSFER STUDENT, ZACK WELLS. I'M MISSING AN IMMUNIZATION SHEET—

—ZACK WELLS. CAPTAIN OF THE FENCING TEAM? LOOKS LIKE HE WAS DEAN'S LIST, TOO.

ADMISSIONS OFFICE

Mrs. Wood

I SEE.

AND YOU DON'T HAVE A FENCING TEAM, EITHER?

ADMISSIONS OFFICE

Mrs. Wood

I SUSPECT THE ERROR IS OURS. AS I SAID, HE'S NEW AND HIS RECORDS ARE INCOMPLETE. POSSIBLY HE'S FROM ONE OF THE OTHER SCHOOLS IN PLANO.

ADMISSIONS OFFICE

Mrs. Wood

I THINK OF CALLING THE DEAN.

I THINK OF CALLING THE POLICE.

THEN I THINK OF POOR ELLIE, WHO HAS HELPED A LOT OF KIDS AND DONE HER BEST TO BE A GOOD MOM TO THAT CHILD OF HERS.

ELLIE DESERVES A CHANCE TO EXPLAIN HERSELF BEFORE I BRING IN THE DEAN.

ADMISSIONS OFFICE

Mrs. Wood

ELLIE WHEDON LOVED LUCAS CARAVAGGIO AND NOW HE'S BACK FROM THE DEAD...

...ALWAYS ASSUMING HE REALLY DIED, AND I THINK THAT'S A SAFE ASSUMPTION. AND SHE'S READY TO RISK HER JOB AND MORE FOR HIM.

CALLIOPE RIDGEWAY

Director Of Admissions
1979 – 2004

You Are Missed

WOULD I DO ANY DIFFERENT IF IT MEANT HAVING YOU BACK?

HELL, NO.

ADMISSIONS OFFICE

Mrs. Wood

I'D DIE TO HAVE YOU BACK. KILL TO HAVE YOU BACK, FOR THAT MATTER.

I NEED TO THINK ABOUT THIS. ABOUT WHAT IT MEANS. ABOUT WHAT HAPPENS NEXT. I NEED A PLAN.

I NEED A DRINK. I'M SCARED. I WISH YOU WERE HERE TO TELL ME WHAT TO DO. I DON'T KNOW WHAT TO DO. OH, CALLIE.

DIDN'T YOU ONCE SAY I WAS THE DUMBEST SMART GUY YOU KNEW?

I'M NOT WORRIED ABOUT WHAT SOLDIER JOE KNOWS. I'M WORRIED ABOUT JOE RIDGEWAY. THE FUCKING DRAMA PROFESSOR.

HE'S FIGURED IT OUT. ENOUGH TO RUIN EVERYTHING. HE KNOWS WE FAKED MY TRANSCRIPT.

OH, SWEET FUCKING HELL.

PRIVATE, BELAY THAT LANGUAGE! WE'RE AMONG CIVILIANS.

WHAT ARE YOU GOING TO DO?

EVIDENCE ROOM
AUTHORIZED PERSONNEL ONLY

WHAT I SAID I'D DO. DEAL WITH IT.

NO ONE ANSWERS THE BELL.

I'M RELIEVED, REALLY. WHAT IF *HE* ANSWERED THE DOOR? WHAT WOULD I SAY, KNOWING WHAT I KNOW NOW?

I SHOULD CALL SOMEONE, DO SOMETHING.

MAYBE—

—NO.

OR—

—BETTER NOT. THINK ABOUT THIS. TAKE A MOMENT.

I'D LIKE ONE MORE SHOT, BUT I'VE PROBABLY HAD ENOUGH.

THE NEXT DRINK IS ON ME, MR. RIDGEWAY.

HELLO, LUKE. ARE YOU GOING TO SHOOT ME WITH THAT RATHER BRUTAL-LOOKING GUN?

I'D RATHER NOT. I WISH YOU COULD'VE LEFT ME ALONE. I ALWAYS LIKED YOU.

HERE. HAVE A COUPLE.

I DON'T THINK SO.

I'VE WONDERED ABOUT YOU, LUKE. ABOUT WHAT HAPPENED TO YOU AND YOUR FRIENDS. THEY WERE GOOD KIDS.

THEY WERE *GREAT* KIDS. RIGHT UP UNTIL THE DAY THEY DECIDED TO KILL ME.

SOMETHING WHICH DIDN'T WORK OUT SO WELL FOR THEM.

DIDN'T WORK OUT SO WELL FOR ME, EITHER, BUT I'M NOT GOING TO DWELL ON IT.

AND IF I CAN'T USE THEM, THEY CAN DIE LIKE YOU.

IT'S NOTHING PERSONAL, BUT NO ONE CAN KNOW ABOUT ME. I JUST CAN'T TAKE A CHANCE ON YOU EXPOSING ME. TAKE YOUR PILL, MR. RIDGEWAY. LET'S DO THIS EASY.

MY GOD. I'VE BEEN HAMLET. A GHOST RIGHT IN FRONT OF ME AND I COULDN'T MAKE UP MY MIND WHAT I OUGHT TO DO.

DON'T GET UP.

THE IMPORTANT THING IS I'M BACK NOW, AND I CAN FINISH SOMETHING— SOMETHING WONDERFUL. SOMETHING THAT NEEDS FINISHING.

THE LOCKE CHILDREN... THIS ALL HAS TO DO WITH THE LOCKE CHILDREN?

IT HAS MORE TO DO WITH THAT HOUSE. AND WHAT'S UNDER IT. THEY'RE JUST THERE. I THINK I CAN EVEN MAKE THEM HELP ME.

HELP ME.

WHAT—WHAT CAN YOU NEED ME FOR?

WAS THERE SHOOTING? I SMELL A GUN.

THE GHOST CODE
Joseph Elmore Ridgeway III

IS HE—

DON'T LOOK IN THERE.

"YOU DON'T WANT TO LOOK IN THERE."

CLIC!

OHMIGOD, YOU'RE BLEEDING.

IT'S NOT BAD. HE HIT ME WITH A GLASS. I'LL CLEAN IT UP BEFORE WE GO.

I NEED YOUR HELP WITH THIS THING. IT'S NOTHING LIKE THE COMMODORE 64 I USED TO HAVE.

I NEED TO GET RIDGEWAY'S COMPUTER TURNED ON AND I WANT TO SEND ONE OF THOSE, WHAT ARE THEY? I-MAILS?

AND I HAVE NO IDEA WHAT TO DO WITH THIS THING.

I HAVE NO CLUE.

WHAT?

HE SENT A MASS E-MAIL TO EVERYONE IN HIS ADDRESS BOOK AROUND EIGHT-THIRTY. WE'VE GOT A PRINTOUT IF YOU WANT TO READ IT.

HE SAID HE COULDN'T LIVE WITHOUT HER ANYMORE. HIS WIFE. SHE DIED OF CANCER A FEW YEARS BACK.

WHEN WE CAN DRAIN THE TUB. DIDN'T YOU JUST ASK ME WHEN WE COULD DRAIN THE TUB?

I DID NOT ASK. BUT THE IDEA CROSSED MY MIND THAT THE WATER MUST BE COLD AND I WOULD LIKE IT IF PROFESSOR RIDGEWAY WAS REMOVED FROM IT NOW. PERHAPS I WAS THINKING TOO LOUDLY.

DID HE MENTION HOW HE CAME TO POSSESS A GUN WITH NO SERIAL NUMBERS?

UH... NO. BUT HE DID QUOTE SHAKESPEARE. WHICH IS CLASS IN MY BOOK.

YOU'RE NOT BUYING IT.

SUICIDES PUT THE GUN IN THE MOUTH. WITHOUT EXCEPTION. AND UNTRACEABLE PISTOLS ARE USED FOR HOMICIDE, NOT FOR SELF-ANNIHILATION.

ALTHOUGH I AM GLAD TO REPORT TO THE PRESS WE BELIEVE THE CAUSE OF DEATH TO BE SUICIDE. THERE IS NO REASON FOR THE PERPETRATOR TO KNOW WE KNOW HE EXISTS.

I'VE... NEVER HEARD ANYONE USE "SELF-ANNIHILATION" IN A SENTENCE BEFORE. THAT WAS COOL.

DETECTIVE?

LOOKEE LOOKEE.

GUESS WHAT?

WHAT? **WHAT?**

YES. I KNOW. I HAD HIM LAST YEAR AND HE WAS MY FAVORITE—

HE JUST **KILLED** HIMSELF?

WHAT THE HELL IS WRONG WITH PEOPLE?

KINSEY, WAIT. LET'S GO IN AND SEE WHAT THEY SAY AT MORNING ASSEMBLY. THEY'RE GOING TO RELEASE EVERYONE AFTER ASSEMBLY ANYWAY TO—

AW, FUCK THAT. JUST FUCK THAT.

SHE TOUCHED ME, MATE. RIGHT HERE.

AND BURST INTO TEARS. YOU THINK MAYBE THERE'S A CONNECTION?

KINSEY LOCKE. THE SLAYER OF SERIAL KILLERS TOUCHED MY HEART. DO YOU KNOW WHAT THIS MEANS?

THAT YOU WERE STANDING IN HER WAY, ASSHEAD?

IT MEANS SHE **WILL** BE MINE.

34

HERE.

HOW'D YOU—

JACKIE SAID YOU HEADED DOWN HERE.

WHAT'S THIS?

YOU'RE A SAGITTARIUS, YOU READ COMICS, AND YOU HAVE A GREEN STREAK IN YOUR HAIR. SO I ASSUME YOU MUST DIG PISTACHIO.

I THINK I HATE PISTACHIO.

TOOK MY BEST GUESS. DON'T LIKE IT? SHOOT ME.

MMM. GIVEN YOUR RECENT HISTORY THAT PROBABLY WASN'T MY BEST CHOICE OF WORDS.

YOU, UH, AREN'T ARMED RIGHT NOW, ARE YOU?

HE'LL SAY ANYTHING.

HIS MOUTH IS THE MOST CHARMING THING ABOUT HIM. FOR ABOUT TWENTY MINUTES. AFTER THAT THE APPEAL KIND OF WEARS OFF.

IT'S REALLY GOOD.

THE ICE CREAM. I GUESS I NEVER GAVE PISTACHIO A CHANCE.

THIS IS SO STUPID. FEELING THIS WAY. I ONLY HAD TWO WEEKS OF CLASSES WITH HIM.

EXCEPT HE HAD THESE BOW TIES. AND I WAS REALLY LIKING HAMLET.

I HATE THIS. I HATE HATE HATE—

WHAT? HAVING FEELINGS FOR PEOPLE?

YEAH. YEAH, THAT.

IF EVEN ONE MORE PERSON I KNOW DIES, I'M GOING TO LOSE MY MIND.

IF YOU DON'T UNLOCK SOMETHING SOON, I'M GOING TO LOSE MY MIND.

OH, GODFRICKINGRRR NOGOODKEYFRIGA DAGIT...

RATTLE
RATTLE
RATTLE
RATTLE

DOESN'T FIT HERE...

HMM. I WONDER.

RRROO

OOOARR

THAT'S MY RIDE YOU'RE SITTING ON.

AAA!

I'M... OH MAN, I DIDN'T MEAN ANYTHING... I WAS JUST... YOU KNOW—

WHATEVER. NO BIG DEAL. I'M JUST NOT WILD ABOUT STRANGE BUTTSWEAT ON MY BIKE.

STRANGE WHAT—I'M... ARE YOU IN MY ETHICS CLASS—YOU ARE! DID YOU...

...DID YOU FINISH THE READING? IT'S... IT'S PRETTY INTERESTING, RIGHT?

IF YOU SAY SO. I HAVEN'T EVEN STARTED YET. TAKE IT EASY, HUH?

YOU'RE GONE.

YEAH. I'M OUT OF HERE.

I'VE GOT TALENTLESS ART STUDENTS TO TEACH IN PROVINCETOWN, AND THERE'S JUST NO WAY TO COMMUTE BACK AND FORTH.

AND YOU HAVE TO GO TODAY. YOU HEARD ABOUT WHAT HAPPENED TO KINSEY'S ENGLISH PROFESSOR?

MR. RIDGEWAY. I KNOW. I'M GOING TO TALK TO HER BEFORE I LEAVE.

OUTSTANDING. I'M SURE ONE TALK FROM YOU WILL SOLVE ALL HER EMOTIONAL PROBLEMS.

I DON'T THINK ANY AMOUNT OF TALKING IS GOING TO SOLVE HER EMOTIONAL PROBLEMS. I THINK LIVING WILL. AND SHE'LL DO THAT WHETHER I'M HERE OR NOT.

THERE WERE SOME PEOPLE WHO SAID IT WAS A BIG RISK, PUTTING SOMEONE MY AGE IN CHARGE OF THE ENTIRE PROGRAM. I DON'T WANT TO PROVE THEM RIGHT BY SCREWING UP MY FIRST YEAR ON THE JOB.

I'LL ONLY BE TWO HOURS AWAY.

BESIDES. BRIAN CALLED LAST NIGHT. HE WANTS TO KNOW IF I'M EVER COMING BACK.

I'VE GOT A LIFE WAITING FOR ME, NINA.

YOU'RE ONE UP ON ME, THEN.

43

ALRIGHT, MAN. IT'S WEIRD SAYING THIS CONSIDERING THE CIRCUMSTANCES... PROFESSOR RIDGEWAY AND ALL... BUT... IT WAS FUN.

FOR REAL.

GUESS WHAT? WE GOT MORE TROUBLE LIKE JOE RIDGEWAY.

FUCKING DUNCAN LOCKE. WE RAN INTO EACH OTHER AND I THINK HE REMEMBERED ME. HASN'T SEEN ME SINCE HE WAS *EIGHT*. HOW THE FUCK DO YOU LIKE THAT?

DAMN. SMELLS LIKE THE FISHSTICKS ARE BURNING.

DON'T DO THAT WITH YOUR HEAD, BODE. I DON'T LIKE IT.

THAT'S IT? "DAMN, IT SMELLS LIKE THE FISHSTICKS ARE BURNING AND DON'T DO THAT WITH YOUR HEAD, BODE? WHAT THE FUCK?"

MOMMMM!

MOM? DID YOU... DID YOU HAVE A GOOD LOOK AT BODE? I MEAN, DID YOU REALLY *LOOK* AT HIM? THAT WASN'T A MAGIC TRICK.

WHAT WASN'T A MAGIC TRICK?

HIS HEAD. HE'S GOT THE TOP OF HIS HEAD OPEN LIKE A MANHOLE COVER.

UH-HUH.

THESE ARE FUCKED.

THINGS ARE LOOKING PRETTY GRIM WITHOUT DUNCAN, GUYS. SOMETIMES I SWEAR THAT MAN HAS THE ENTIRE *CHEF'S BIBLE* FILED INSIDE HIS HEAD.

MAYBE I CAN DO A QUICK ALFREDO.

IT'S LIKE SHE KNOWS BUT DOESN'T CARE.

KNOWS BUT DOESN'T CARE? HIS HEAD IS OPEN!

OPEN AND *COMPLETELY* EMPTY!

OKAY, ACTUALLY THAT LAST PART MAKES SENSE.

IT ISN'T EMPTY! LOOK INSIDE!

IT'S ALL TRUE. SAM LESSER... THE CRAZY THINGS SAM BELIEVED ABOUT SECRET KEYS... IT'S—

YEAH. YEAH, IT IS.

THE NIGHT SAM SHOWED UP, I THOUGHT I DIED.

BUT REALLY, I WENT THROUGH THE DOOR BODE TOLD US ABOUT. THE ONE THAT TURNS YOU INTO A GHOST.

LATER, I TOLD MYSELF I PASSED OUT WHEN SAM WAS CHOKING ME AND IMAGINED THE REST. BUT I KNEW I WAS LYING TO MYSELF ALL ALONG.

GUYS! THIS GETS WAY COOLER! JUST *LOOK* IN MY HEAD!

ALL RIGHT. I WILL IF YOU WILL.

GUUUUUHNNNH

OKAY. LET'S DO IT.

WHAT ARE YOU DOING?

YOU CAN PUT THINGS IN. I WONDER IF YOU CAN TAKE THINGS OUT.

... WHILE THE FETTUCCINE IS COOKING, WHISK TOGETHER THE CREAM, BUTTER, DIJON...

WHY WOULD YOU WANT TO TAKE THINGS OUT?

TO LOOK AT THEM. BODE SAID HE MET THIS SCARY GHOST GIRL IN THE WELLHOUSE. I WANNA SEE HER.

...OVER LOW TEMPERATURES. REMOVE FROM HEAT WHEN THICKENED. DO NOT BOIL...

C'MON, YOU LITTLE BITCH... GOT HER!

AUUGH!

IS THAT WHAT SHE LOOKED LIKE?

BODE? IS THIS WHAT YOU SAW IN THE WELLHOUSE, THE NIGHT SAM LESSER SHOWED UP HERE?

AUUGH!

W-WHAT THING IN THE WELLHOUSE? I NEVER SAW ANYONE IN THE WELLHOUSE. DID I?

WHAT DO YOU *MEAN* YOU NEVER SAW ANYONE IN THE WELLHOUSE? YOU'VE TOLD US A THOUSAND TIMES—

UH... KINSEY? HE PROBABLY DOESN'T REMEMBER SEEING HER IN THE WELLHOUSE BECAUSE YOU JUST TOOK THE MEMORY OF HER OUT OF HIS HEAD.

HMM. POSSIBLY.

THAT'S THE SCARIEST, MOST FUCKED-UP-LOOKING BEAST I'VE EVER SEEN.

I WONDER.

WONDER WHAT?

I WONDER IF THAT'S THE WAY SHE LOOKED, OR IF THAT'S JUST THE WAY BODE RECALLS HER. REMEMBER, HE ONLY SAW HER ONCE, AND IT WAS DARK, AND HE WAS TERRIFIED.

YOU'RE PUTTING HER BACK?

OF COURSE. IT'S HIS MEMORY. HANG ON, THOUGH. I WANT TO SEE—

GAAH! WHAT THE HELL IS *THAT*?

I THINK IT'S MRS. MAYHEW. REMEMBER THE OLD WOMAN WHO LIVED DOWN THE ROAD FROM US IN WILLITS? SHE SCREAMED AT BODE FOR WALKING ON HER LAWN?

OH, YEAH. SCARED THE HELL OUT OF HIM. BUT SHE DIDN'T LOOK LIKE THAT...

...MUCH. I MEAN. THE WHISKERS ARE RIGHT.

I'VE HEARD MEMORY IS UNRELIABLE. I GUESS IT'S TRUE.

CAN YOU CLOSE YOUR HEAD NOW, BODE?

TAK

CLIC

CAN I SEE THE KEY?

OKAY. BUT I WANT IT BACK.

I FOUND IT IN THE POOL OUT—

I DON'T CARE WHERE YOU FOUND IT. YOU DON'T TELL ANYONE ELSE ABOUT THIS. AND DON'T TALK TO MOM ABOUT IT.

TALKING ABOUT KEYS IS ONLY GOING TO GET HER UPSET, AND SHE CAN'T SEE WHAT IT DOES, ANYWAY. THIS IS OUR SECRET. NO ONE ELSE KNOWS ABOUT IT EXCEPT YOU, ME, AND TYLER.

HEY! IT'S MINE! I FOUND IT!

GIVE IT BACK.

KEEP YOUR SHRIEKY LITTLE VOICE DOWN, DINK. YOU'LL GET IT BACK.

WE JUST WANT TO CHECK IT OUT. MAKE SURE IT'S SAFE.

63

THAT THING IN THE WELLHOUSE... SAM CAME HERE TO SET HER FREE.

HE WAS AFTER TWO KEYS. ONE OF THEM WAS TO LET HER OUT AND I DON'T KNOW WHAT THE OTHER ONE WAS FOR.

DO YOU THINK THIS IS THE OTHER KEY SAM WANTED?

NAW. NOT THAT ONE. SAM SAID IT WOULD HAVE AN OMEGA SYMBOL ON IT. I GOT THAT MUCH.

THERE'S A BUNCH OF THESE KEYS FLOATING AROUND THIS PLACE. THE GHOST KEY. THAT ONE. WHO KNOWS HOW MANY.

SO THIS THING THAT WAS OUT IN THE WELLHOUSE, SHE'S STILL OUT THERE SOMEWHERE. AND SHE STILL WANTS ONE OF THESE KEYS. AND SHE COULD SHOW UP AT ANYTIME TO GET IT.

MOM LOOKED RIGHT INTO BODE'S HEAD, OPEN LIKE A BUCKET, AND JUST WANDERED OFF.

MOM NEEDS TO KNOW.

IF SHE DIDN'T BELIEVE THAT, WHEN IT WAS STARING HER RIGHT IN THE FACE, THEN SHE ISN'T GOING TO BELIEVE WE MIGHT BE ATTACKED BY BODE'S HOMICIDAL ECHO.

YOU BELIEVE HOW WARM IT IS? IT STILL FEELS LIKE SUMMER.

"REMEMBER DAD USED TO MAKE US GO OUTSIDE IN THE SUMMER AND LIE DOWN IN THE GRASS TO LOOK AT THE STARS?

"HE TOLD MOM IF ANYTHING EVER HAPPENED TO US, WE SHOULD COME HERE. TO LOVECRAFT. TO KEYHOUSE. THAT WE'D BE SAFE HERE."

WHEN DID HE SAY THAT?

A LONG TIME AGO. LIKE A PART OF HIM KNEW... SOMETHING. I DON'T KNOW WHAT.

IT'S HARD TO SEE HOW COMING HERE HAS MADE US SAFER.

MAYBE HE MEANT "SAFE" IN RELATIVE TERMS. BECAUSE... BECAUSE OF ALL THESE OTHER KEYS.

MAYBE DAD WANTED US TO HAVE A CHANCE TO FIGURE OUT HOW THEY WORK. WHAT THEY'RE FOR. MAYBE THERE'S A WAY TO USE THEM TO FIGHT—WHATEVER IT IS THAT'S OUT THERE.

RIGHT. THIS IS WHAT I'VE BEEN THINKING. WE HAVE THIS THING, AND WE BETTER FIGURE OUT HOW TO USE IT TO OUR ADVANTAGE.

BODE HAD HIS TURN TO MESS AROUND WITH IT. NOW IT'S TIME TO TEST IT OUT ON US.

TAK

CLIC

UH... STRIPPED FROM HIS POSITION IN 1512, MACHIAVELLI WAS FORCED... BLAH BLAH... FORM A NEW UNDERSTANDING OF POLITICAL POWER... YADDA YADDA... BIG HEN CLASSIC EDITION.

...$4.50 IN THE U.S., $6.99 IN CANADA. I EVEN KNOW THE ISBN NUMBER ON THE BACK COVER.

SO DID THAT WORK? DO YOU KNOW ANYTHING ABOUT MACHIAVELLI?

DO YOU WANT TO TRY?

ANYTHING YOU EVER WANTED TO KNOW... ALL WE GOT TO DO IS POP YOUR HEAD OPEN AND PLOP IT IN THERE.

NO. I MEAN...

...I'M NOT SURE I WANT TO PUT THINGS IN.

I DON'T KNOW. I CAN'T THINK ANYMORE.

I'M GLAD WE HAD A CHANCE TO TALK WITHOUT BODE. AFTER WHAT HE'S BEEN THROUGH, I DON'T WANT HIM PANICKING ABOUT THE RETURN OF THE WELLHOUSE LADY.

I WISH THERE WAS SOMEONE WE COULD TALK TO ABOUT...

NO! HEY, LOOK. AT LEAST UNTIL WE KNOW MORE, WE BETTER KEEP THIS BETWEEN US.

OH, ABSOLUTELY. I'M JUST THINKING ALOUD. I MEAN, HONESTLY. WHO DO YOU THINK I'M GOING TO TELL?

- LORD OF THE FLIES
- MACHIAVELLI

The Ethics of Many

The Ethics of the Individual

MR. LOCKE? MR. LOCKE?

TYLER?

THE FLIES
AVELLI

The Ethics of Many

The Ethics of the Individual.

HUH? WHAT? YES! I AGREE.

THAT YOU NEED MORE TIME TO FINISH THE READING?

AH, YES. YES. I MEAN, NO! I'M FINE. I FINISHED THE READING YESTERDAY.

BOTH BOOKS? EXCELLENT.

THEN I'LL BE EXPECTING YOUR ESSAY NEXT MONDAY AS WELL, ALONG WITH EVERYONE ELSE'S.

GOOD LUCK EVERYONE. HAVE A GREAT WEEKEND.

HOW DID YOU FINISH BOTH BOOKS, AMIGO? YOU HADN'T EVEN STARTED YESTERDAY. I BEEN READING ALL WEEK AND I'M ONLY HALFWAY THROUGH *THE PRINCE*.

AT LEAST YOU'VE READ HALF. I HAVEN'T EVEN STARTED. AND THERE'S NO WAY IN HELL I CAN FINISH BOTH BOOKS THIS WEEKEND.

I KNEW I SHOULD'VE DROPPED THIS COURSE. PERSONAL ETHICS ARE WASTED ON ME ANYWAY.

YOU OUGHTA TEACH ME YOUR SPEED-READING METHOD ONE OF THESE DAYS, TYLER.

YEAH. SERIOUSLY.

Head Games
Chapter Two

LOCKE & KEY
Created by Joe Hill and
Gabriel Rodriguez

Written by JOE HILL
Illustrated by GABRIEL RODRIGUEZ
Colored by JAY FOTOS
Lettered by ROBBIE ROBBINS
Edited by CHRIS RYALL

HOW ABOUT TONIGHT?

BOOOOMM

SHHHHAAAAAAAAAA

GAHDAKDAK

...SURE IT'S SAFE?

... WHOLE POINT OF GETTING THE VALVES OPEN. THE LOWER BARRACKS OUGHT TO STAY DRY, EVEN DURING HIGH TIDE.

I'M STILL GOING TO FEEL BETTER WHEN WE'RE OUT OF HERE. THEY DON'T CALL THIS THE DROWNING CAVE FOR NOTHING.

LET'S DO IT, THEN.

HEY, GUYS... WE'VE GOT COMPANY.

PROVINCETOWN, MASSACHUSETTS—NOW

IT'S TERRIBLE, WHAT GETTING OLD DOES TO PEOPLE. THEY DON'T JUST GET UGLIER ON THE *OUTSIDE.*

THIS DIDN'T HAVE TO HAPPEN TO YOU, YOU KNOW. GETTING OLD. IF YOU HAD JUST STUCK WITH ME AT THE END, WE COULD'VE—

—AH. WELL. YOU DON'T REALLY REMEMBER. HERE. TAKE THIS.

I'M GOING TO TRY AND HELP YOU. SOMEHOW. YOU'RE NO USE TO ME IF YOU GO CRAZY.

AND YOU'D BE NO GOOD TO RUFUS, EITHER. YOU WANT TO THINK ABOUT THAT. IF YOU HAVE A NERVOUS BREAKDOWN, WHO'S GOING TO LOOK AFTER YOUR SON?

ME?

"WHAT DO YOU THINK YOU'RE *DOING?!*"

WHAT TOOK YOU SO LONG? IT'S LATE.

AUNT ELLIE SHOVED A BUNCH OF HOT CHERRY PIE IN MY FACE AND WOULDN'T LET ME GO UNTIL I ATE MYSELF SICK. WOMAN CAN COOK.

OKAY FOR YOU TO SPEND THE NIGHT?

SURE. I HAVE THAT LADY UNDER MY POWERS.

SO WHAT'S THIS AMAZING THING YOU JUST HAD TO SHOW US ON A FRIDAY NIGHT AND HOW'S IT GOING TO HELP US GET A'S?

IT'S, UH, IT'S PRETTY INTENSE. PROBABLY THE MOST INTENSE THING EITHER OF YOU HAVE EVER SEEN.

AND THEN HE UNZIPPED HIS PANTS.

AHHWHAT?

NEVERMIND. KEEPING MYSELF ENTERTAINED. GO AHEAD. SHOW US YOUR THING. OR—*ER*—WHATEVER IT IS YOU WANTED TO SHOW US.

RIGHT. I'M GLAD YOU GUYS CAME OVER. I THOUGHT SOMEONE BESIDES US HAD TO KNOW ABOUT THIS.

THIS IS GOING TO BE... A LITTLE SHOCKING.

CL IC

81

WAIT—DON'T GO. I KNOW THIS IS FREAKY AND—

—NO ONE WITH HALF A FUCKING BRAIN WOULD JUST DROP THIS ON YOU—

JORDAN? ARE YOU OKAY?

DO YOU WANT ME TO CLOSE MY HEAD?

JORDAN! WAIT!

HOW THE HELL DID YOU THINK SHE WAS GOING TO REACT, DUMBASS?

LET GO, I NEED TO—

YOU NEED TO PUT ON THE TOP OF YOUR HEAD BEFORE YOU TRY TALKING TO HER.

I THOUGHT SHE'D THINK IT WAS WILD... I THOUGHT... I MEAN...

...I WAS GOING TO ASK HER TO A MOVIE BUT NOTHING GOOD WAS PLAYING.

HERE. TAKE IT.

I... I DON'T KNOW WHAT TO SAY. WHAT YOUR BROTHER JUST DID—WAS THAT SOME KIND OF DOUG HENNING STUNT?

DOUG HENNING?

Y'KNOW. THE MAGICIAN WHO DOES THE TV SPECIALS.

LIKE CRISS ANGEL? OH. NO. IT WAS REALLY REAL.

CLIC

WHERE DID THIS COME FROM?

HERE. KEYHOUSE. WE THINK IT'S JUST ONE OF MANY. THAT THERE ARE OTHER KEYS IN THIS HOUSE THAT DO OTHER THINGS.

IT'S A LONG STORY. IT ACTUALLY STARTS BACK IN SAN FRANCISCO, WITH WHAT HAPPENED TO MY DAD. AND IT'S... IT'S ALL PRETTY CRAZY.

I JUST WATCHED YOUR BRO OPEN HIS HEAD LIKE A TRASHCAN. LAY IT ON ME.

JORDAN! WAIT! DON'T GO!

STOP. HANG ON.

I SHOULDN'T HAVE... BUT IT'S JUST... WELL WHAT WOULD YOU DO—IF YOU HAD SOMETHING SO AMAZING? I MEAN, YOU'D HAVE TO SHOW *SOMEONE*—AND I DON'T KNOW ANYONE...

...AND... IT'S HARD TO SAY ALL THIS WHEN I CAN'T SEE YOUR FACE.

I DON'T KNOW WHAT YOU DID IN THERE, BUT I CAN TELL WHEN I'M BEING FUCKED WITH AND I DON'T LIKE IT.

LET GO OF MY ARM. *NOW.* I'M GOING THROUGH A LOT OF SHIT RIGHT NOW AND I HAVE BETTER THINGS TO DO WITH MY FRIDAY NIGHT THEN HANG OUT WITH A COMPLETE FREAK.

...SHE'S HALF OUT OF HER MIND, SHE'S SO ANGRY. WHO WOULDN'T BE? AND THE OTHER THING IS HOW MUCH NINA DRINKS NOW...

WHILE WE HAVEN'T BEEN DRINKING NEARLY ENOUGH.

...I KNOW I NEED TO BE *HERE*, BUT I JUST FEEL LIKE...

QUIT IT, ALREADY. THEY CAN LIVE WITHOUT YOU. WHEREAS...

...I KNOW I CAN'T. AND I'M FUCKALL WHEN IT COMES TO SHARING.

HEY, BRI—THERE'S A CLUB UP THE BEACH THAT MIGHT BE—

—PLAYING CHER OR SOME OTHER SHIT I DON'T WANT TO LISTEN TO. IF WE'RE GOING TO HAVE A BEER, I WANT TO DRINK SOMEPLACE WHERE WE CAN WATCH THE GAME.

C'MON. LET'S GO HOME.

NAH. YOU ARE ENTIRELY TOO SOBER.

IT'S DARK DOWN HERE.

COME ON, KID. I'LL SEE YOU PART OF THE WAY BACK.

WHERE ARE YOU GOING? I WANT TO GO WITH YOU.

THEN WHY ARE YOU GOING?

CAN'T. IT ISN'T SAFE.

BECAUSE IT ISN'T SAFE. THAT'S THE FUN. IT'S A BIGGER KID THING.

BUT TAKE IT FROM YOUR BUDDY, DODGE. IT WOULDN'T BE FUN IF SOMETHING HAPPENED TO YOU. HEAD ON BACK, OKAY?

OH, AND HEY, IF ANYONE ASKS WHERE WE WENT...

...FORGET YOU SAW US DOWN HERE, OKAY?

I JUST CAN'T GET OVER THIS. THIS IS... BEYOND BELIEF.

www.freedom.org

I MEAN, THINK OF THE POSSIBILITIES. IF LEARNING ANYTHING WAS AS EASY AS TURNING A KEY IN A LOCK, WHAT WOULD YOU WANT TO LEARN?

YOU COULD KNOW IT ALL. EVERY PHILOSOPHICAL WORK EVER WRITTEN. CUTTING EDGE MATHEMATICS.

THE SECRETS OF THE WORLD'S BEST ALLIGATOR WRESTLERS.

YES! NOW YOU'RE TALKING.

IT'S NOT JUST WHAT YOU CAN PUT IN. IT'S WHAT YOU CAN TAKE OUT.

LIKE TAKE OUT WHAT?

YOU KNOW THE AWFUL THING IN THE WELL THAT KINSEY TOLD YOU ABOUT? THE THING SAM LESSER WANTED TO SET FREE?

KINSEY PULLED IT OUT OF MY HEAD TO LOOK AT IT!

SHE... SHE DID? WHAT'D IT LOOK LIKE?

TRY AND IMAGINE A CROSS-DRESSING VAMPIROBITCH WITH SNAGGLY, NASTY TEETH AND A GREEN, DEAD FACE. THEN TAKE WHATEVER YOU'RE IMAGINING AND MAKE IT TEN TIMES UGLIER.

LIKE ALL *RAWWWWR GAAARKH...*

THAT BAD, HUH? CROSS-DRESSING VAMPIROBITCH?

WELL. MAYBE SHE FELT PRETTY ON THE INSIDE.

TRUTH IS, SHE COULD'VE LOOKED LIKE ANYTHING. TURNS OUT WHAT YOU REMEMBER AND WHAT YOU IMAGINE GET PRETTY MIXED UP IN THERE.

AHH. I'D KNOW HER IN A SECOND IF I EVER SAW HER AGAIN.

LIKE WHAT?

ANYWAY. I'M LESS INTERESTED IN EXTRACTING MEMORIES THAN I AM IN... GETTING RID OF SOME OTHER JUNK.

FEAR. I WANT TO TAKE OUT THE FEAR THAT'S IN THERE.

AND I'D LIKE TO FORGET HOW TO CRY. I AM SO FUCKING SICK OF CRYING.

I DON'T KNOW IF THAT'S SUCH A GOOD...

I NOTICE YOU DON'T ASK ME FOR PERMISSION BEFORE GOING AHEAD WITH *YOUR* STUPID IDEAS. GO ON.

YOU'VE GOT TO DO THE HONORS. I THINK IF I REACH INTO MY OWN HEAD I'LL SCREAM. OR WEEP.

CLIC

YEAH, WELL, IF EVERTHING GOES RIGHT, WHEN I'M DONE YOU WON'T WANT TO DO EITHER.

TAK!

I'M NOT SURE WHAT I'M LOOKING FOR...

THERE! THAT'S IT.

RIGHT. YEAH. SHIT. SLIPPERY BASTARD. SOMEONE GET SOMETHING TO PUT IT IN.

AH! LOOK AT IT! NASTY LITTLE FUCKER!

DON'T LET IT GO!

WAIT. I THINK... GOT THE OTHER ONE!

WELL GET RID OF 'EM!

HOLD UP THAT BOTTLE!

GOT HIM. WE NEED SOMETHING TO STICK IN THE BOTTLE.

YAAAA! STAB STAB STABBEE STABSTAB! YOU'RE GOING TO DIE OF GANGRENE IN THE THUMB!

BOB MARLEY DIED OF CANCER IN HIS FOOT! IT COULD HAPPEN!

HEY, KINSEY, YOUR UNCLE DUNK'S PICTURE GOT SMASHED.

NICE PLACE. THIS WHERE HE WAS GOING WHEN HE PULLED OUT THE OTHER DAY?

YEAH. HE RUNS AN ART PROGRAM IN PROVINCETOWN.

HE DOESN'T HAVE A GIRL IN HIS LIFE?

AH... NO. NOPE. HE'S JUST, YOU KNOW... YOUR BASIC PERMANENT SINGLE GUY.

HOW DO YOU FEEL?

LIKE ANYTHING COULD HAPPEN AND THAT WOULD BE ALL RIGHT. LIKE THE NEXT THING THAT HAPPENS WILL BE A CHRISTMAS PRESENT. GOOD. BAD. WHATEVER. I CAN'T WAIT TO OPEN IT.

YOU OUGHT TO GET RID OF THESE THINGS YOURSELVES... YOUR FEAR AND YOUR TEARS.

THINK ABOUT IT. YOU'VE GOT ONE OF THEM IN YOUR HEAD ALL THE TIME, TELLING YOU LIES AND STABBING YOUR BEST SELF.

YOU'VE GOT THE OTHER DROWNING YOUR THOUGHTS IN UNHAPPINESS. TELL ME HOW THEY DO YOU ANY GOOD.

YOU'RE BLEEDING.

OH. RIGHT. HE SHIVED ME A COUPLE TIMES.

HEY, LOOK. IT'S A LITTLE FACE. I THINK MR. THUMB IS SURPRISED.

OKAY. YOU'RE RIGHT. I MAY NEED TO LAY BACK DOWN.

CHRIST. THE ROOM IS STILL MOVING. I DIDN'T THINK I WAS THAT DRUNK.

YOU WEREN'T. THAT'S PUNCH-DRUNK.

TELL YOU WHAT. WHY DON'T YOU TAKE TWO ASPIRIN FOR YOUR BANGED-UP SKULL, AND TWO MORE FOR YOUR HEAD FULL OF CRAZY.

WHAT'S THE BET YOU DON'T EVEN REMEMBER THIS CONVERSATION TOMORROW?

SNNNKKK- SNORK. SNK.

OR YOU COULD JUST PASS OUT. WHATEVER WORKS. LEAVING ME BRUISED, SAD, AND LONELY.

AT LEAST THERE'S BEER IN THE FRIDGE.

♪ HIGH TIME, DRAW THE LINE... ♪

...PUT AN ENNNND TO THIS GAAAME BEFORE IT'S TOOOO LATE... ♪

AMMO #17

cic!

TAK!

HI, DUNCAN. DON'T DO ANYTHING STUPID. LET'S NOT WAKE THE NEIGHBORS WITH A LOT OF SCREAMING AND SHOOTING.

WAKE UP, ALREADY!

SHE CAN'T HEAR YOU.

SHIT.

WAKE UP, GODDAMN IT, HE'S COMING BACK!

HE'S HERE! HE'S HERE AND HE'S NOT WHO YOU THINK HE IS!

ZACK?

SORRY... I WOKE UP AND FOR A MINUTE I THOUGHT... I THOUGHT IT WAS ALL A DREAM. TYLER OPENING THE TOP OF HIS SKULL, AND YOU TAKING THOSE LITTLE CRITTERS OUT OF YOUR HEAD, AND ALL THE REST OF IT.

I PROBABLY SHOULDN'T HAVE COME IN YOUR ROOM. DIDN'T MEAN TO WAKE YOU UP. I JUST NEEDED TO SEE THEM AGAIN. SEE IF THEY WERE REAL.

WHAT ARE YOU DOING?

STOP. DON'T.

HM? STOP ME YOURSELF, WHY DON'T YOU? SHOVE ME AWAY. SCREAM. FIGHT. DO *SOMETHING*.

2:24 AM

YOU'RE HAVING FUN WITH ME. YOU KNOW I CAN'T.

IT'S LIKE THE OTHER TIMES. I'VE TRIED, I'VE TRIED TO—

"TRIED WHAT, ELLIE? WHAT HAVE YOU TRIED TO DO?"

RollingStone
The Year In Music

"HURT ME? RUN AWAY?"

"NOT MUCH LUCK WITH THAT, HUH?"

"I TRIED TO WARN JOE RIDGEWAY YOU WERE COMING TO KILL HIM. BUT I COULDN'T DIAL HIS NUMBER. EVERY TIME I TRIED I GOT..."

...MOVIEFONE! PRESS '1' TO HEAR SHOWTIMES FOR G.I. JOE: THE RISE OF COBRA! PRESS '2' TO HEAR SHOWTIMES FOR TERMINATOR: SALVATION...

"OH, ELLIE. THAT WASN'T A SMART IDEA. IT'S A GOOD THING THERE'S BEEN A PIECE OF ME INSIDE YOU, TO PREVENT YOU FROM DOING ANYTHING SO STUPID AND SELF-DESTRUCTIVE.

"IF YOU WEREN'T USEFUL TO ME, WHY WOULD I LET YOU AND RUFUS LIVE?"

WHA-AT? WHY WOULD YOU KILL RUFUS? HE'S NEVER DONE ANYTHING TO HURT YOU...

BUT YOU HAVE. I'D DO IT JUST TO MAKE YOU WATCH. I HAVEN'T FORGOTTEN WHAT SIDE YOU CHOSE IN THE END, ELLIE. EVEN IF YOU DON'T EXACTLY REMEMBER.

HONESTLY, PLAYING WITH YOUR OLD AND TIRED MEAT AND YOUR OLD AND TIRED EMOTIONS IS SO MUCH FUN, I'D MUCH RATHER KILL HIM THAN YOU.

IT'S SAD, REALLY. YOU USED TO KNOW... WE ALL USED TO KNOW... THERE'S NOTHING MORE PATHETIC THAN GROWN-UPS. THEY'RE SO EASY TO USE. AND DESTROY.

YOU DIDN'T HAVE TO GET OLD. YOU HAVE NOBODY BUT YOURSELF TO BLAME FOR YOUR SAGGING TITS, AND THAT USELESS CHILD OF YOURS, AND YOUR INABILITY TO COPE WITH MAGIC.

WHAT ARE YOU DOING? I'M AFRAID.

DON'T BE. THAT PART OF ME THAT'S INSIDE YOU? THAT'S BEEN KEEPING YOU IN CHECK? I'M ABOUT TO TAKE IT OUT. I'M GIVING YOU BACK YOURSELF.

ISN'T THAT NICE OF ME? WHAT DO YOU SAY, ELLIE? C'MON. LET'S HEAR IT.

THANK YOU.

YOU'RE SURE IT'S NO TROUBLE? I... I DIDN'T KNOW MY MOM WAS GOING TO CALL AND BOTHER YOU.

IT WASN'T ANY BOTHER. YOUR MOM HAD MY PARENTS' PERMISSION TO CLAM SOGGY COVE SINCE BEFORE I WAS BORN. SHE PROBABLY HAS MORE RIGHT TO IT THAN I DO.

THAT KEY OPENS THE FRONT DOOR OF THE HOUSE AS WELL AS THE GATE. IF YOU NEED TO GET WARM, GO AHEAD AND LET YOURSELF IN.

NO, I... I WOULDN'T LIKE TO DO THAT. I HAVEN'T BEEN IN THERE SINCE I WAS A KID. THAT'S YOUR PRIVATE SPACE.

OH, YOU WON'T BOTHER ME. I'M OUT OF HERE, ANYWAY. DOING TURKEY DAY IN PROVINCETOWN WITH BRIAN.

THIS THAT SAME GUY?

YEAH, I CAN'T SEEM TO GET RID OF HIM.

I'LL SEE YOU, ELLIE.

OH, AND YOU AND YOUR MOM BE CAREFUL ON THE STEPS LEADING DOWN TO THE BEACH. THEY GET WET AND SLIPPERY. SOMEONE'S GOING DOWN THEM HEADFIRST ONE OF THESE DAYS.

I SWEAR, THOSE STAIRS HAVE BEEN WAITING TO KILL SOMEONE SINCE THEY WERE CARVED OUT OF THE ROCK.

LOVECRAFT—BEFORE

FILTHY LITTLE SODOMITE.

SNOBBY LITTLE RICH BOY.

MOTHER. PLEASE. HE CAME ALL THE WAY OUT HERE SO WE COULD—

GET DOWN ON BENDED KNEE AND KISS THE ROSY RING OF HIS ASS.

HARD TO SEE WHAT WE'RE UP AGAINST IN ALL THIS ~KAUGH KAUGH~ SMOKE!

DANGER. ENVIRONMENTAL SENSORS REPORT ~KAUGH KA-KAUGH~ THE PRESENCE OF TOXINS HARMFUL TO HUMANS.

LOOKED DOWN ON ME SINCE HE WAS LITTLE. IT RUNS IN HIS FAMILY. THE LOCKES ALWAYS HAD A HIGH OPINION OF THEMSELVES.

I WASHED THEIR LINENS FOR 20 YEARS. WASHED THE STAINS OUT OF HIS SHITTY DIAPERS, TOO. I DOUBT IF HE EVEN KNOWS MY FIRST NAME.

MOM, PLEASE. I TOLD YOU WHAT THE DOCTOR SAID ABOUT RUFUS'S HEART, AND I ASKED YOU VERY NICELY NOT TO SMOKE IN—

MY OWN DAMNED HOUSE? LAST I CHECKED, MY NAME IS STILL ON THE DEED, AND I'M NOT DEAD YET. MUCH TO YOUR REGRET, I'M SURE.

DON'T WORRY. I'LL CROAK SOON. THEN YOU CAN AIR THE PLACE OUT TO YOUR SATISFACTION.

~KAUGH KAUGH~ NUTS TO THAT. GONNA TAKE MORE THAN A LITTLE ~KAUGH~ TEAR GAS TO PUT ME DOWN.

FAR AS THAT GOES, IF BEING AROUND ME DON'T SUIT HIS ENVIRONMENTAL SENSORS, MAYBE HE'S THE ONE OUGHT TO MOVE ALONG. THERE'S HOMES FOR THEM, YOU KNOW.

THEM?

HE'S FOURTEEN. THAT'S OLD ENOUGH TO LEARN HOW TO DO SOMETHING USEFUL. THEY TEACH 'EM A TRADE.

PUMP GAS. HE'D ENJOY THAT, I IMAGINE. JUST LIKE PLAYING WITH HIS TRUCKS. BE GOOD FOR HIM.

BE GOOD FOR YOU, TOO. MAYBE YOU COULD STOP HIDING BEHIND HIM AND GET A MAN BACK IN YOUR LIFE.

GO TO BED, MOM. YOU'RE DRUNK.

OH, NOT YET. I'M AFRAID YOU'RE HEARING THE VOICE OF SOBRIETY. BUT GIVE ME TIME. I'LL GET THERE.

I'M NOT AFRAID TO GO BEHIND ENEMY LINES. I'M NOT AFRAID.

YOU'RE NOT GOING ANYWHERE. YOU UNDERSTAND THAT, RUFUS? IT'S YOU AND ME, KID.

I'D SEND HER TO A HOME BEFORE... WHATEVER.

I JUST WANT THE COMMANDER TO KNOW IF SHE'S EVER TIRED OF ME, THE TEAM WILL MOVE OUT AT HER COMMAND. SAY THE WORD.

NEGATIVE. YOUR MISSION IS TO STAY HERE AND DEFEND THE BARRACKS. DO YOU COPY THAT?

COPY THAT.

GOOD. TIME TO TUCK IN, KID. THIS IS CURFEW.

YOU THOUGHTLESS BITCH.

MM. UNH.

SNNK-SNORK!

I FEEL LIKE WE NEVER TALK ANYMORE.

SOMETIMES I THINK YOU'RE ONLY INTERESTED IN ME FOR THE SEX.

THERE'S BEEN A DISTURBANCE IN THE BARRACKS.

GAAAAAAH—DAMN IT! RUFUS!

GO TEAM RESPONDED TO A DISTRESS CALL AND DISCOVERED A LEAK IN THE BUNKS.

HE MEANS THE RETARD PISSED HIMSELF AGAIN.

RUFUS! DON'T CALL YOURSELF THAT. I WON'T HAVE THAT TALK IN THIS HOUSE. YOU UNDERSTAND ME?

MA'AM, YES, MA'AM. THERE'S A HOLE IN THE WALL OF THE BATHROOM. WAS THERE AN ARTILLERY STRIKE?

NO. I'LL FIX IT. CLOTHES OFF AND IN THE SHOWER, KIDDO. MOM WILL CHANGE YOUR SHEETS AND THEN BACK IN BED.

YES MA'AM. THE ROOKIE IS WONDERING IF YOU'LL LAY WITH HIM AFTER HE HOSES OFF. THE... THE KID IS SCARED OF THE DARK.

FUCKING THING.

HA! FUCKING THING! I MADE A PUN. JOE RIDGEWAY WOULD LIKE THAT ONE.

OH, FOR CHRIST'S SAKE, WHERE THE HELL DID YOU FALL, YOU FRIGGING—

—HUNH?

TOK TOK TOK

TOK TOK TOK

COMING.

JACKIE. THANKS FOR GIVING ME ONE OF YOUR SUNDAY MORNINGS. I KNOW RUFUS WILL BE EXCITED TO SEE YOU.

I'M READY FOR HIM. LITTLE LANEY DOES LOVE A MAN IN A UNIFORM.

YOU HAVE FUN. SO YOU AND YOUR MOM ARE GOING CLAMMING?

FOR THE THANKSGIVING STUFFING. IT'S AN... OLD YANKEE THING.

ARE WE GOING?

I THOUGHT YOU WERE MAD.

RUFUS SAID IT WAS AN ACCIDENT.

WELL. TRUE ENOUGH.

COME ON, MOTHER. IT MIGHT SNOW LATER. I WANT TO GET THIS OVER WITH.

WELL? DO IT IF YOU'RE GOING TO DO IT.

HAH.

UNH. UH. UNNH.

TALKING TO YOURSELF, ELLIE?

YOU'VE BEEN HANGING AROUND RUFUS TOO MUCH.

OR ARE YOU THINKING YOU OUGHT TO LEAP IN THE WELL? STOP KIDDING YOURSELF. IF YOU DON'T HAVE THE GUTS TO GET RID OF ME, YOU DON'T HAVE THE GUTS TO GET RID OF YOURSELF.

'COURSE IF YOU DID JUMP, I COULD FINALLY PUT THAT RETARDED—

SHUT UP ABOUT HIM. SHUT UP ABOUT HIM OR I SWEAR—

OH, PLEASE.

GET YOUR FINGER OUT OF MY FACE, YOU LITTLE BITCH.

YOU DON'T HAVE ANYTHING TO THREATEN ME WITH.

I WISH YOU HAD'VE KIL'T ME. THEN I COULD'VE DIED KIDDING MYSELF MY DAUGHTER HAS A LITTLE SPINE.

BUT IF YOU HAD ANY SPINE AT ALL YOU WOULDN'T BE CLINGING TO THAT HALF-WIT, USING HIM TO AVOID HAVING A LIFE.

135

AND IN A WAY, IT *DIDN'T* HAPPEN. THE POLICE, THE DOCTORS... EVERYONE BELIEVED YOU WHEN YOU TOLD THEM YOUR MOTHER FELL DOWN THE STEPS TO SOGGY COVE.

HELL, BY THE TIME YOU GOT TO THE HOSPITAL, THAT'S WHAT YOU REALLY THOUGHT HAPPENED. IT WAS SIMPLE ENOUGH FOR THIS OLD MEMORY OF MINE TO WORK INSIDE YOUR HEAD, MANIPULATING YOUR THOUGHTS.

BESIDES, YOU DIDN'T WANT TO KNOW THE TRUTH.

THIS PART OF ME THAT'S BEEN INSIDE YOU HAS BEEN MORE HELPFUL THAN YOU COULD EVER IMAGINE.

WORKING IN YOUR HEAD TO KEEP YOU FROM KNOWING THINGS I DON'T WANT YOU KNOWING. HOLDING YOU IN CHECK BY SWAPPING BANANAS FOR KNIVES AND MIXING YOU UP WHEN YOU DIAL THE PHONE.

SHAME I HAVE TO TAKE HER OUT, BUT YOU'RE NO GOOD TO ME CRAZY, AND SHE'S DEFINITELY DONE A LOT OF DAMAGE IN THERE.

I BETTER TAKE OUT ALL THE OTHER THINGS YOU REMEMBER ABOUT ME, TOO. LIKE THE MAN SAYS ON TV: EVERYTHING MUST GO!

I AM SORRY I HAVE TO DO THIS, ELLIE. I KNOW SOME OF THOSE MEMORIES WERE SPECIAL.

OKAY, KIDDING. I'M REALLY NOT SORRY. YOU WERE FUCKING MAKING ME NUTS CALLING ME "LUKE" ALL THE TIME.

THE ONLY THING I'M SORRY ABOUT IS THAT I HAD TO WAIT A YEAR TO GET OUT OF THE WELLHOUSE. I WISH YOU COULD'VE HELPED ME WITH THAT, BUT IT WAS SAFER FOR YOU NOT TO KNOW TOO MUCH.

AND I FIGURED PEOPLE WERE GOING TO HAVE TO DIE AND THAT YOU WOULDN'T HAVE THE STOMACH FOR THAT.

SPEAKING OF SAFETY, I GUESS I'M BETTER OFF IF RUFUS DOESN'T KNOW SO MUCH ABOUT ME, AS WELL.

I REALIZE NOW I'VE BEEN CARELESS AROUND HIM. LETTING HIM SEE MAGIC. LETTING HIM HEAR TOO MUCH ABOUT WHAT I'M GOING TO DO.

NO! LEAVE RUFUS ALONE... WHOEVER... WHOEVER YOU ARE.

I DON'T THINK THERE'S MUCH CHANCE HE COULD HURT ME, BUT BETTER SAFE THAN SORRY.

NO! PPPPLLÉAAS...

SHHH. HUSH NOW. IT WON'T MATTER IF THERE'S A LITTLE LESS IN RUFUS'S HEAD.

YOU REST NOW. DREAM HAPPY DREAMS. I'M GOING TO WRITE UP SOME FAKE MEMORIES AND STICK 'EM IN YOUR SKULL.

WHEN YOU WAKE UP, IT'LL BE LIKE NONE OF THIS EVER HAPPENED. YOU'LL REALLY BELIEVE I'M THE COUSIN YOU'VE BEEN TELLING EVERYONE I AM.

I'M GOING TO FIX YOU, ELLIE.

RIGHT AFTER I FIX RUFUS.

2:33 AM

OKAY, YOU BIG STUPE. LET'S SEE IF THERE'S EVEN ANYTHING IN THERE TO—HUNH?

WHAT THE—?

WHERE'S THE FUCKING KEYHOLE? THERE'S ALWAYS A—

WELL, IT... IT CAN'T MATTER.

PROBABLY HEADS WITH NOTHING IN THEM CAN'T OPEN. FUCK IT.

NEVER MIND. HE'S NOTHING.

YOU'VE GOT THINGS TO DO. MEMORIES TO CREATE. KEYS TO FIND. LEAVE IT.

THAT WAS CLOSE. *TOO* CLOSE.

WE MUST BE ON GUARD. THE REPLICANT COULD BE THE GREATEST ENEMY WE'VE EVER FACED. HIS CAPACITY FOR CRUELTY IS IMMEASURABLE.

YEAH, WELL. IF HE THINKS ANY OF US IS GONNA RUN WITH OUR TAILS BETWEEN OUR LEGS, HE'S GOT ANOTHER THING COMING. AIN'T THAT RIGHT, BOYS?

aNYWHeRe KeY

us'd the key to anyplaice againe, to return to Boston, & gaither intelaigents for Crais. Tis an act of terryble wychcraift, but better I do it, than my sister, who is obssaissed with REVENGING herself upon the RED-COATS, for thair violence agin our faither & brother & belov'd maither. Aye, my dredd of beeing called to acconnt someday by SATAN HIMSELF is a trifling concern when maiched with my desyre to rid the worlde of the devylls who taik the King's Coyne to do raip & murdur...

HeaD KeY

of alle the keys I have forged from the WHISP'RING IRON, 'tis the key that opens the human mind I most regrait. Miranda hast a pervairse fasinaytion whist the key & hast us'd ait to fill her head with all thair is to know about WAR & the SLAIYING of MEN, & she carrys an arsanall whist her whairever she goes. Yet I am less in dred of what she has put in than what she hast remov'd. Sometimes it is as if she is now without FEER and indeed is herself more man than I!

GeNDeR KeY

my sister - or should I now say my brother! - fights the shadow war with Crais in the streets of Boston whilst I wait at home, like a helpless maiden, praying to the ALLMAIGHTY! for her safe return. When first I fashin'd the key, I imagained she maight trainsform to a boy to protect her, if necessaire, from the unsavorie lusts of ENGLISHMEN should the King's foot-soldiers return to Lovecraft to abuse God fairing womain. Never did I think she wouldst WILLENGLY caist off the wardrobe of her femininitie for this ruggaid liberation among men...

ECHO KEY

whence I unlock'd the dore I heerd a voice that saimed to ecko from the well & it aisk'd me who I sot & I spake of my brother. No sooner had the words pass'd my lips thence he ROSE from the WELL like a spairt & yet was living flaish, alltho he had dyed in the Drowning Caves not 6 weeks beefor. He clasp'd me to his bosom & sayd why do ye look so unhappy to see me brother, but I wast in feer for my allmaighty SOUL & fled to the howse & pray'd thair to the LORD

But in that grait howse, an ecko of my voice was all the reeply I receiv'd

GHOST KEY

onlee in occaisonull daith do I find peece now, for with the bode caste aisyde, it is possibull for one to know his own ETERNAIL SOULE. My spairt cannot leeve the grounds of Keyhowse, but heyre I walke laik an aingel! I aim everywhare and nowhare at once, from the tall's towair, to the deepst caves. It is hard to dreem thair could be any dore more terryble or wondairfulle than that wych dyvydes deth from lyfe, yet my expairances at the thraishold of the black dore have teach'd me thair are worse things than to dyye...

OMEGA KEY

in our
& I resolve
hazzarded such a
long I work'd in
till finallie t'was
oh how I feer'd!
in the gatho
struiked ou
held the
beigd
Gon
ho

THE KNOWN KEYS
(EXCERPTS FROM THE DIARY OF
BENJAMIN PIERCE LOCKE, 1757 – 1799)

Series Illustrator and co-Creator Gabriel Rodriguez, for the first time, shares the process involved in developing a page of Locke & Key.

Step 1: The Script

Once a script is received, I read it two or three times, completely, BEFORE I start drawing. I'm used to receiving a new script when I'm finishing the previous issue, so this reading process is useful for me to start turning words into images, still free from the problem of drawing. It also helps me to identify the easy, the not so easy, and the extremely hard pages and sequences. Having done this mental exercise, I'm ready to face the white page.

Step 2: The Page Script and Documentation

Here we'll follow the creation of page 8, from *Locke & Key: Head Games* #6 "Army Of One." I start re-reading (again) the description of the page and the text that it will have in it. Having previously pictured it in my mind, I know the elements involved, and start imagining them turned into a comic panel.

I try to turn the visual concept into a specific shot.

During this process, I identify elements that demand research or the collection of references, external references, and elements that appear early in the story. In this scene, the key elements are: a mason jar (fortunately, I had one at hand here at home), the two keys (check *Locke & Key: Welcome to Lovecraft* #6), female Dodge's dress (check in *Welcome to Lovecraft*, too) and the shape of the hole in the bathroom wall (check early pages of this same issue). Having all those elements at hand, I know I'm able to create an image consistent with the story, and with the visual appeal we have developed for our tale.

On this specific page there is a particularly complex element: What does a hand look like holding a mason jar like the one Ellie is supposed to be holding? This kind of uncommon relation between body and object is a key element of establishing believable body language for the characters. I solve the problem by looking at photos in books, or sometimes by watching myself in the mirror, but in this case I held a mason jar in my left hand, at an angle like the one I'll draw, while working on the next step.

Step 3: Rough Line Work

The first step of drawing, finally... I try to do a fast and very synthetic, but as definitive as possible, organization of all the elements of the image. This is a chance to define the camera shot, angle, and balance between elements. In this case: Ellie, shocked, watching the mason jar; the jar, the note outside the jar, the little She Dodge, the Well Key, the note attached to the Well Key, the Gender Key, the wall, and the hole in the background. The idea here is trying to solve the outlines and overlapping of elements, the sense of space, the body language and expression of the characters, and the dramatic feeling of the scene.

Step 4: Final Pencils

The second step of drawing consists of simultaneously correcting any deficient element from the previous step, while adding, as completely as possible, the remaining graphic elements that will compose the scene.

In this particular panel, being a splash page that we want to be shocking and spectacular, I try to do detailed pencils for the complete image. Also, because I have to deal with elements of different scale that require different approaches, it is important, for example, to have a detailed perception of Ellie and her reaction, in an extreme close up, and at the same time from She Dodge, which has a small full-body shot. Here we also balance the thickness of lines to distinguish elements, and the relation of visual weight between full blacks and the rest of the line work. All this, considering that we can still make changes with the inking.

In pages with more panels, I usually don't have time to do this complete, detailed penciling. In those, I try to select the most complex elements and develop them in full detail, while elements that are easier to solve directly with the inking remain schematic.

Step 5: Main Outlines

The process of inking starts with drawing the main outline shapes of the different elements included in the shot. At this stage, the priority is working on the characters and most important objects, while the background just needs detailing on some key lines and, sometimes, the main full-black elements (on some occasions this is left for the final step, depending on the relation between elements and background...). It's important here to identify the different objects and characters clearly, and also to establish the outline of the overlapping elements, which is crucial when you're dealing with translucent objects, like the mason jar.

Step 6: Detailing Characters

It's important to give the proper relevance to the main elements of the image, in this case the characters and the keys. So, their full inking is the next step, to have it solved before inking the other elements. That helps when you need to change some details in the background inking in order to keep the relevance of the main visual elements. Also, in this example, it is time to solve one of my regular nightmares in the inking process... the HAIR. Sometimes I wish I only had to draw bald people...

Step 7: Detailing Background and

Step 3

Step 4

Step 5

Step 6

Step 7

Step 8

Remaining Elements

And this is how we complete the handwork of the inking process, aware that there may still be some things to polish. But fortunately, we still have a post-production stage...

Step 8: Scanning and Cleaning the Lines

This is a crucial stage. We start scanning the page as a color file. Then, manipulating brightness and contrast of the image, we enhance the inking. After that, we turn the file into a CMYK color file. Next, we select the yellow channel of the color file (which shows only clean elements from the black layer of the image) and create a new file, this time in B&W, without any trace of the blue pencil lines. In this file the black lines appear gray, so we adjust the brightness and contrast of the image to get the traditional full black. Now we're almost done.

Step 9: Post-Production and Definitive File

And then we have the final lines... or do we? When we get to this part of the drawing with just the inked lines, it's common to notice some details that don't work as well as we would want. I used to repeatedly make the mistake of drawing more lines than necessary, and some elements would not look exactly as we wanted. So we have a cleaning process (in this case removing some

extra lines from Ellie's face, hands, and lips), and

another round of adjusting details (correcting some lines in the faces of the Gender Key, reducing Dodge's smile a little, and fixing the hole of the paper attached to the Well Key, which looks like an extra "o" in the original drawing). Having this done, we copy this drawing into the official page format and "voilá!" We have our finished inks ready to be delivered.

Steps 10, 11, and 12: Approval, Coloring, and Lettering

The last three steps are the ones that continue after my work. Once delivered, the page needs to be approved by the writer and editor. Once given the okay, the editor uploads the file on the FTP server, and from there the color artist grabs the file to proceed with the digital coloring. Once Jay's wonderful work is done, the pages are uploaded back to the server, now in full color, to be approved by editor, writer, and artist. After that, Robbie proceeds with the lettering, then it's sent to the writer for revisions, specifically to see if the text needs any changes...

And THEN, we've got a finished page, ready to go to print.

Repeat this process about 22 times (sometimes more), and you have what you need to produce a cool comic book.

—*Gabriel Rodriguez*

ART
GALLERY

BY GABRIEL RODRIGUEZ

is the author of a novel, *Heart Shaped Box*, and a collection of stories, *20th Century Ghosts*. He is currently at work on a new novel. The worst comic book he ever read was still a pretty good time. He has a website, joehillfiction.com, where you can find out stuff; you can also follow him on Twitter where he goes by the inspired handle of joe_hill.

is a supremely gifted Chilean artist and co-creator of the twisted but wonderful world of *Locke & Key*. The invitation to participate in the fantastic journey of the surviving members of the Locke family, conceived by Joe Hill, has become a dream project made real for Gabriel. He asks that readers unlock their hearts and minds, and accept an invitation into new realms and tales, thrilling experiences, and secret places that his efforts craft into a vivid universe.

In addition to his current work in *Locke & Key*, Gabriel has collaborated with IDW on *Clive Barker's The Great And Secret Show*, *Beowulf*, *George A. Romero's Land of the Dead*, as well as several *CSI* comics. He currently lives in Santiago, Chile, with his wife, Catalina, and their sons, José Manuel and Matías.